DATE DUE	
NOV 17 1995	
APR 2 0 1996	
MAY 1 8 1996	
OCT 1 6 1996	
NOV 0 6 1996	
AUG 2 8 1997	
JUN 1 6 1998	
JUL 3 1 1999	
OCT 0 2 1999	
NOV 2 5 2003	

GAYLORD   PRINTED IN U.S.A.

Fish in a Flash!

Fish in a Flash!

A Personal Guide to Spin-Fishing

BY JIM ARNOSKY

Bradbury Press • New York

Collier Macmillan Canada • Toronto
Maxwell Macmillan International Publishing Group
New York • Oxford • Singapore • Sydney

To Glad and Charlie Fox

Bradbury Press
Macmillan Publishing Company
866 Third Avenue
New York, NY 10022

Collier Macmillan Canada, Inc.
1200 Eglinton Avenue East
Suite 200
Don Mills, Ontario M3C 3N1

First edition
Printed in the United States of America
1   2   3   4   5   6   7   8   9   10

The text of this book is set in 12 point Cheltenham Book.

About the full-color fish portraits: All of the fish, except the brown trout,
were caught with spinning tackle by the author especially for this book.
The freshly caught fish were held in an aquarium and drawn from life,
then quickly returned to their native waters. Back home, in his studio, Jim
Arnosky added the natural colors of each fish to his drawings, using first
a watercolor wash, followed by a layer of colored pencil. He then finished
each drawing with soft black pencil.

Book design by Jim Arnosky

Library of Congress Cataloging-in-Publication Data
Arnosky, Jim.
Fish in a flash! : a personal guide to spin-fishing /
by Jim Arnosky. — 1st ed.
p.   cm.
Summary: An introduction to the techniques and joys of the most
popular method of fishing in the world, one which uses lures that
spin, wobble, and flash.
ISBN 0-02-705854-9
1. Spin-fishing—Juvenile literature.   [1. Spin-fishing.
2. Fishing.]   I. Title.
SF456.5.A76   1991
799.1′2—dc20   90-45832   CIP   AC

c.1

Contents

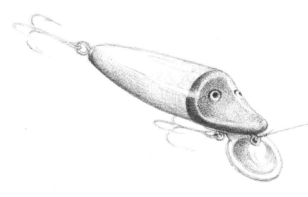

Introduction

Of all the methods of fishing with rod and reel, spin-fishing is the most recent. Spin-fishing began in Europe in the 1940's, shortly after World War II. In a few years it had spread to the United States. Today it is the most popular method of fishing in the world, in both freshwater and saltwater. Spin-fishing is easy to learn, fun to do, and it catches fish!

With this book you will learn to use spinning tackle. I'll show you ways to make a rubber worm swim like a snake, a metal spoon wobble like a tadpole, a spinner flash silver or gold like a shining minnow, and a wooden plug swim and dart in the water like a frog.

Most of my fishing is done in freshwater streams, ponds, and lakes. But you can use my methods and techniques along with your own spinning gear wherever you fish, in inland or coastal waters. Even in the deep sea. And believe me, you will catch fish, from trout in cold streams to bass in weedy ponds to bluefish in the rolling surf. In spin-fishing there are no nibbles or nudges. Fish strike spinning lures suddenly and vigorously. In the flash of an instant, you are on to your quarry.

So come along! It is a good day to go fishing. You needn't bring a thing this trip. I'll share my tackle, my know-how, and some cherished memories along the way.

Jim Arnosky
RAMTAILS, 1991

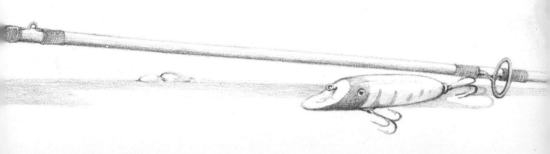

Chapter 1
Spinning Tackle

A spinning rod is light and simple—just a six- or seven-foot rod with a cork handle. The reel is attached to the cork handle with two *O* rings or aluminum bands that slide over the reel's seat-plate (that part of the reel that *seats* on the rod handle). The spinning reel is positioned below on the rod handle. On even the most inexpensive spinning reels, the crank handle can be switched to the right or left side of the reel, so that a right-handed person can comfortably cast with the right hand and reel in with the left. A left-handed person casts with the left hand and reels with the right. Line is stored on an open-faced stationary spool. During casting, the spool's open face allows line to spill off the spool. To prevent the line from spilling off the spool while fishing, there is a wire bale to hold the line. In order to free the line for casting, the wire bale must be flipped out of the way. As soon as the cast is completed, the bale can be flipped

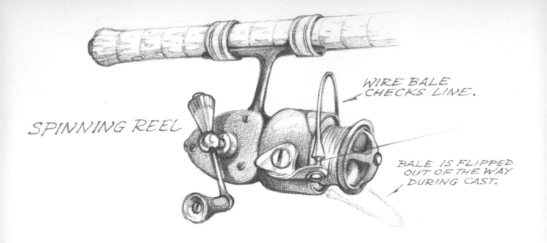

SPINNING REEL

WIRE BALE
CHECKS LINE.

BALE IS FLIPPED
OUT OF THE WAY
DURING CAST.

back in place with one turn of the crank handle
to halt the line.

Spincasting is a version of spin-fishing devel-
oped in the United States by Lloyd Johnson, a
tool and die maker and avid fisherman. The spincasting reel is an enclosed version of the spinning reel. A metal or plastic housing fits over the
spool, and the line, which still spirals off the
spool as in spinning, feeds through a small opening in the housing. Spincast reels are used with
bait-casting rods. The most significant difference
between the spinning reel and the spincast reel

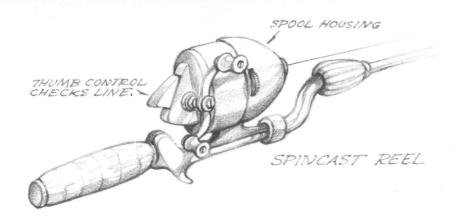

SPOOL HOUSING

THUMB CONTROL
CHECKS LINE.

SPINCAST REEL

is that the spincast reel seats on top of the rod, just the way a bait-casting reel does. Instead of a wire bale to keep the line in check, the line is controlled by a thumb-controlled locking mechanism. Because the enclosed spool helps prevent the line from tangling, and the thumb control to lock and release the line is so simple to use, even very young children can master spincasting on a first outing. However, for sensitivity, pinpoint casting accuracy, and the ability to cast very small lightweight lures long distances, nothing can beat the open-faced spinning reel.

Rainbow Trout ~ 9" length
caught in the Waits River ~
using a small spinner
EA·1990

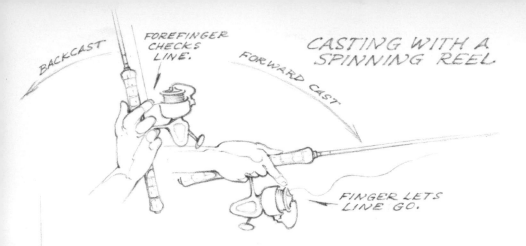

BACKCAST

FOREFINGER
CHECKS
LINE.

FORWARD CAST

FINGER LETS
LINE GO.

ATTACH
LURES
USING
A
CLINCH
KNOT.

Compared to other methods of fishing, spinning tackle is least expensive. A spinning or spincast outfit purchased in a discount store will work just as well as any high-priced equipment, providing it is used with quality line and lures. Cheap line will snap even when new, and poorly made lures will not create the proper action in the water to attract fish.

Monofilament fishing line is a miracle of chemistry. The stuff is thin, flexible but not elastic, and incredibly strong. It also resists deterioration from sun and water. Because monofilament line becomes transparent underwater, it is virtually invisible to fish. You can buy monofilament in two-, four-, six-, eight-, ten-, twelve-, fifteen-, twenty-, twenty-five-, or thirty-pound test strengths. Six-pound test is suitable for most fishing, and it is light enough to throw even the smallest spinning lures. With a six-pound test line—and using the drag mechanism on your spinning reel, which allows a running fish to pull line off the reel without breaking it—you can play and catch fish weighing much greater than six pounds.

Because a spinning reel spins the line as it reels it in, an inevitable twisting occurs. Too much twist makes monofilament line loop and curl, eventually becoming tangled and knotted. To reduce line twist, a snap swivel should be tied to the end of the line and the lure snapped onto the swivel rather than tied directly to the line. Snap swivels work like tiny safety pins, opening and locking closed with just the press of a finger. With a snap swivel on the end of your line, you can change lures instantly, without having to cut the line and tie a new knot.

The lures used in spin-fishing vary greatly in shape, size, and action. I'll tell you about them all in the next chapters. For now, however, you're set with rod, reel, line, and snap swivel. The only other equipment you need includes a pair of needlenose pliers to bend down hook barbs to make them safer to use and to remove hooks from the mouths of fish. You'll also need a nail clipper to cut line, a small plastic tackle box to carry lures, a landing net, insect repellent, and sun-blocking cream. Even if you wear a hat, sunlight reflecting off the water into your face can burn your cheeks and nose.

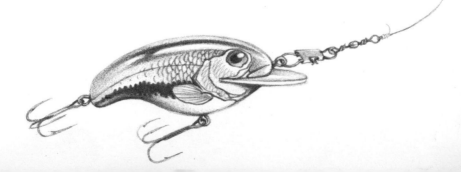

Chapter 2
Spinning in Streams

One June afternoon while fishing in the always muddy Winooski River, I hooked six large rainbow trout, each one outdoing the next in aerial acrobatics. Six fish, one after another, leaping, shaking, flashing in the sunlight, mesmerizing me to the point of distraction, causing that momentary slackness in the line, at which point each fish threw my hook. Frustrating? Yes. Exhilarating? Yes. For a few brief but brilliant moments, I felt as if I were on each fish's back, holding fast to its slippery sides as we both plunged and thrashed in the roily river.

The lure I was using was a small spinner. Small or large, all spinners are made the same way. Treble (triple) hooks are attached to a length of wire. Slid onto the wire, there is a body made of aluminum or plastic for weight and a shiny metal blade for action. When a spinner is pulled through the water, the blade spins around the wire shaft and flashes brightly, like a small baitfish swimming and sparkling in the penetrating sunlight. Besides mimicking a minnow, the spinner's twirling blade produces sonic vibrations that attract fish. Reel a spinner in quickly and it will run shallow. Reel it in slowly and it will sink and run down deep.

Spinners are the most effective spinning lures for fishing in fast-moving streams. Trout or bass holding behind stream boulders often get only a glimpse of passing minnows and will strike at the slightest glint of a shining body. In small streams that measure only twenty or so feet across at their widest, use small spinners. In rivers, larger spinners work best. Always cast your spinner across the current. As soon as the blade hits the stream, begin to reel the spinner back. You will see the blade spinning and flashing as the spinner works its way crosscurrent. A fish may strike it at any time, so be ready to raise your rod and set the hook in an instant. Keep reeling and be alert, especially as the spinner begins to swing around into the current. During this swing, 90 percent of fish strikes occur. If no fish strikes during the swing, let the spinner complete its trip downstream, where it can hold steady in the flow. At this point, you needn't reel to make the spinner blade twirl. The current pressing against the spinner will keep the blade twirling. Any fish close enough to see the flashing metal blade may strike. If, after a little while, no fish strikes, begin to reel the spinner slowly upcurrent, pausing every foot or so to give any fish a longer look. If still no fish strikes, continue to slowly reel the spinner in. I have had fish take a spinner just as I was reeling it up to meet my

FOR SMALL STREAMS
THE PLAINEST-LOOKING
SPINNERS WORK BEST.

rod tip. If no fish has struck by the time you have reeled your spinner in, cast across the current and start the trip again.

Sometimes a spinner will get caught on a stream boulder. When this happens, walk downstream from the snagged spinner so the current can help loosen the hooks and then gently tug until the spinner is free. Do this carefully, so you won't spook fish and spoil the fishing in that spot.

In deep pockets or pools where a stream's larger fish lurk, you can fish a spinner in a variety of ways to try and tempt a big fish into striking. Fish a stream pool first from a downstream position, casting your spinner to the head of the pool or even into the falls spilling into the pool. Begin reeling as soon as the spinner hits the water, slowly at first to present the flashing lure to the fish in the head of the pool—the pool's deepest part. Then reel the lure through the center of the pool all the way to the tail of the pool, increasing your reeling speed as the spinner nears you. This will make your lure appear to be a small fish that might have accidentally tumbled into the pool, swimming quickly to escape the foreboding water. To fish a pool from the side, cast across the current, reel slowly until the spin-

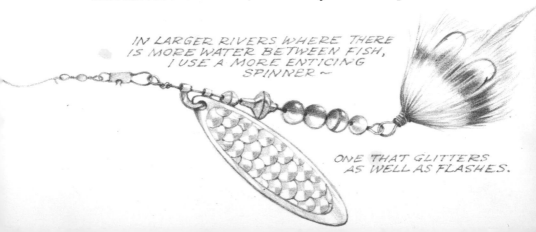

IN LARGER RIVERS WHERE THERE IS MORE WATER BETWEEN FISH, I USE A MORE ENTICING SPINNER ~

ONE THAT GLITTERS AS WELL AS FLASHES.

ner swings into the current, and then begin reeling more rapidly. Again, as you reel your lure up-current, be prepared for the strike of a fish all the way home to your rod tip.

Finally, you can stand upstream of a pool, flip your spinner into the head of the pool, and reel it against the strong flow of entering water. Stop reeling every so often to let the spinner drift with the current and sink a little; then, using short tugs with your rod, jig it back up against the current. This method is especially successful in teasing a strike out of big brown trout that lurk under the ledges below a falls.

Early one evening, I was spin-fishing in a river pool just below a great falls. The water thundering over the falls was digging out a wide hole in the stream bottom. And this hole, so deep and dark and mysterious, was home to a number of

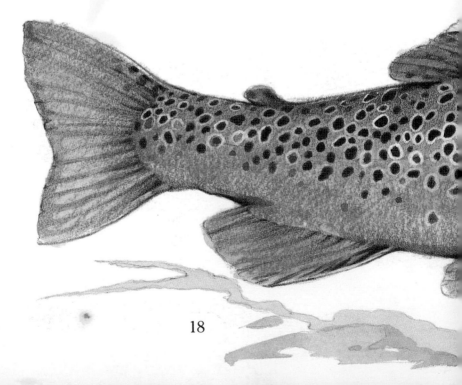

enormous brown trout. The water in the hole swirled and frothed. All around the falls, a vaporous mist rose in the air. I cast a small gold-bladed spinner into the head of the pool and watched as it was first pummeled by the falls, and then as it slowly sank into the abyss. Suddenly I felt a yank, then a powerful tug, and in the black pool I saw the golden form of a brown trout, at least two feet in length. The enormous trout arced its body in an effort to free itself from the metal lure. For a second, the fish resembled a giant yellow banana underwater. In my excitement, I yanked upward with my rod and pulled the lure out of the big trout's mouth. Instantly, the trout was gone, skulking back down under in the dark deep pool. My heart was pounding in my chest so hard that I could hear it above the roar of the falls.

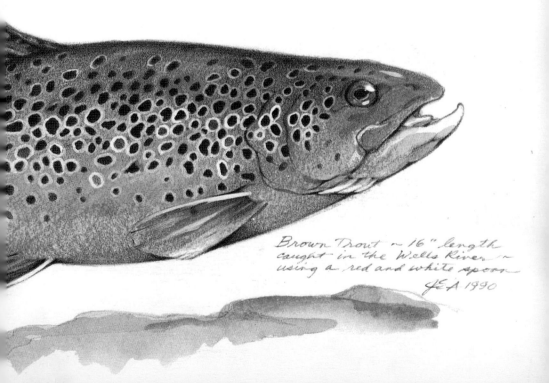

Brown Trout ~ 16" length caught in the Wells River ~ using a red and white spoon
JEA 1990

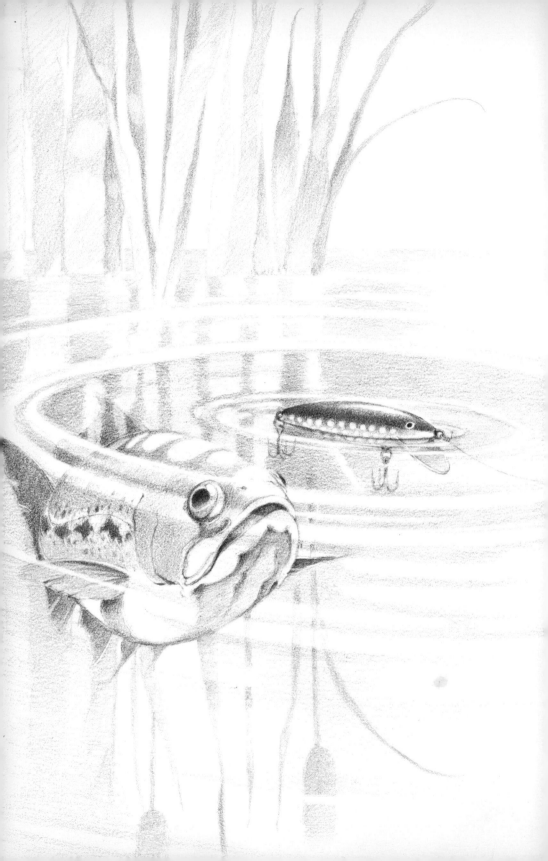

Chapter 3
Spinning in Lakes and Ponds

A stream has places to go, things to do. There is a bed to be dug, banks to be shaped, and obstacles to be undermined and worn away. Compared to a stream, a stillwater pond or lake is a lazy place. The stillwater fisherman casts into a dreamscape of reflected earth, sky, sun, moon, and stars. Only the fisherman's lure plopping into the water ripples the calm. Beneath the calm, however, the chase is on. Big fish are hunting down and gobbling up little fish. Anything that resembles a small fish, even momentarily, stands a chance of being attacked. This explains why, with few exceptions, spinning lures are designed to mimic the looks and actions of small fish.

Spinners work as well in still water as they do in moving water. In lakes and ponds, I use much larger spinners than those I use in streams. Larger spinners are heavier and can be cast farther. And in lakes where the fish can see fishermen through the glassy surface, you want to be able to cast far enough away from yourself to get the fish interested in the lure before it is reeled close enough to where the fish can see you. Also, large spinners can be seen at a greater distance by fish cruising by.

If you are fishing in shallow water, you will want to fish just below the water surface. Begin reeling the spinner in as soon as it plops into the water. If you are fishing in deep water and want the spinner to run down deep, after the spinner hits the water wait one second for each foot of descent you want the lure to sink. Then begin reeling in. Always work the lure all the way in. Unlike in streams where fish lurking behind boulders or holding steady in the current will lunge at a spinning lure only if it passes near them, in still water fish often follow a lure a long way. Sometimes a fish will follow a lure right up to the rod tip before finally snatching it.

My favorite spinning lure for stillwater fishing is the spoon. The story goes that spoon lures were invented by a man who, having lunch in his

Brook Trout ~ 9½" length ~ caught in
a woodland pond~using a small spinner
SD 1990

boat, happened to drop a silver eating spoon into the lake. As soon as the spoon began to sink, a monster muskellunge rushed up from the depths and grabbed it. Like the eating utensil it is named for, a fishing spoon is a metal object concave on one side and convex on the other. Spoon lures vary in size, shape, and color. When reeled through water, a spoon lure wobbles in a way most seductive to fish—especially big fish. As with any lure, the more slowly you retrieve a spoon lure, the deeper it will run. While spinners can be reeled in rapidly and still work effectively, spoon lures will wobble at just the right rhythm to attract fish only when reeled in as slowly as possible, without having the lure sink and snag on the pond bottom.

And as the original spoon fisherman discovered, the flip-floppy way a spoon sinks just after it hits the water will sometimes stimulate a ferocious strike.

Some spoon lures are stamped out to resemble fish shapes. Others are imprinted with details of fish, such as eyes, gill covers, and scales. There are even spoons that have photographic reproductions of various species of baitfish silk-screened on the convex side of the lure. Take it from me: The less a spoon lure looks like an actual fish, the more attractive it will be to the fish. In fact, the most effective spoon lures are those that look like the eating end of table-spoons.

I prefer plain metal spoons, silver, gold, or copper in color. Silver works best on overcast days, when you need all the flash you can get to attract fish. Gold is ideal for normally sunlit days. And copper is the color for extremely bright sunny days, to cut down on too much flashing, which often frightens rather than attracts fish. The only painted or patterned spoons I buy are the red-and-white ones. These tried and proven lures are painted red on the convex side with an S-shaped stripe of white longways down the center. They are plain silver or copper metal on the concave side. No one knows why the "red-and-whites" work so well in attracting fish. I believe the color pattern suggests blood streaming from a wounded baitfish. In fact, the fish these lures attract most are large, exclusively flesh-eating types. For instance, more northern pike have been caught on red-and-white spoons than on any other lure. The largest northern pike I have ever caught—eight pounds, thirty-two inches long—was hooked on a red-and-white spoon. The pike was released; I kept the lure.

Spoons can also be fished with a strip of latex or pork rind attached to the hooks to add a fish-teasing wiggle to the spoon's normal wobble. On windy days, when the water is not so still, both spoons and spinners will catch fish as long as they are fished well under the waves.

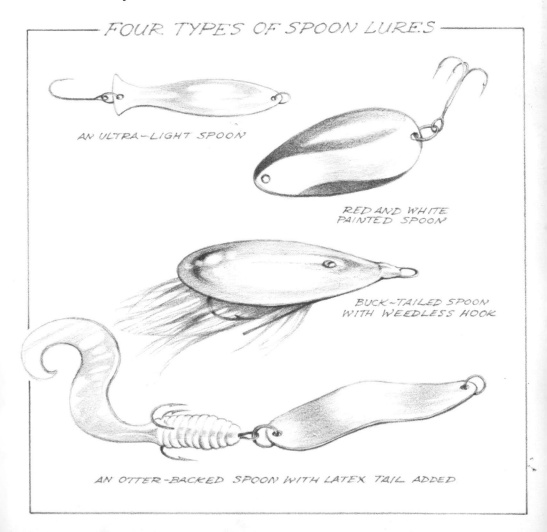

FOUR TYPES OF SPOON LURES

AN ULTRA-LIGHT SPOON

RED AND WHITE PAINTED SPOON

BUCK-TAILED SPOON WITH WEEDLESS HOOK

AN OTTER-BACKED SPOON WITH LATEX TAIL ADDED

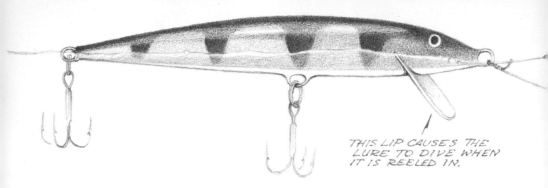

THIS LIP CAUSES THE LURE TO DIVE WHEN IT IS REELED IN.

Floating-diving lures such as the balsa wood or plastic minnows, stick-type plugs, and vamp-styled lures are designed to imitate the actions of wounded minnows. A wounded minnow floats to the surface, jerks a little, twitches, dives in an attempt to swim, only to lose power and rise helplessly, to float once again on the surface. This is exactly the way to fish a floating-diving lure. Cast to a spot where you think a big hungry fish may be lurking underwater. Let the lure float awhile. By tugging the line slightly with your rod, give the lure a jerk. Twitch it. Then reel fast so that the lure dives and swims a few feet. Stop reeling and let the lure rise back up to the surface and repeat the dying scene all over again. When a big fish discovers a wounded minnow, it will swim up to watch the minnow go through its

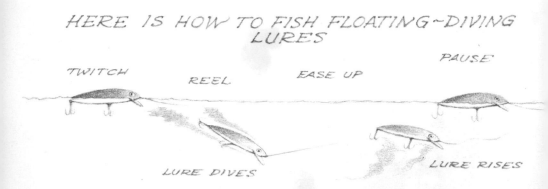

HERE IS HOW TO FISH FLOATING~DIVING LURES

TWITCH   REEL   EASE UP   PAUSE

LURE DIVES   LURE RISES

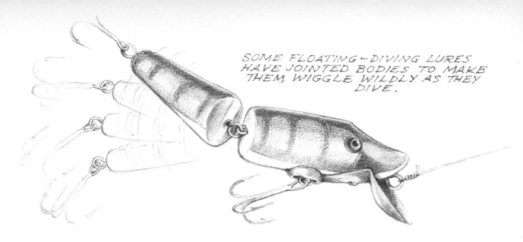

SOME FLOATING-DIVING LURES HAVE JOINTED BODIES TO MAKE THEM WIGGLE WILDLY AS THEY DIVE.

death throes, then suddenly slash upward to nab it. If you happen to see a fish appear suddenly beneath your floating-diving lure, wait a second or two, then give the lure a single twitch. And *bam*! You'll have your fish.

Lures that hit the water, sink, and dive deeply as they are being reeled in are called deep-running lures. There are deep-running lures fashioned to be mistaken by fish for large minnows, small sunfish, fat tadpoles, and even crayfish. I use a deep-running lure that is supposed to look like a big minnow except for its bright fluorescent orange color. Down deep, where little light penetrates, the fluorescent paint glows, and the lure can be seen by fish swimming in the darkness.

TIE LINE DIRECTLY TO DIVING LURES AND OTHER SURFACE LURES. SNAP-SWIVELS WILL HINDER LURE ACTION.

All of the lures I've discussed so far—spinners, spoons, floating-diving, and deep-running—are visual attractors. Fish have to see them flashing, wobbling, jerking, twitching, or wriggling in order to be stimulated into striking. Because of this, all of the above-mentioned lures are most effective when used during daylight hours. Even the fluorescent-colored deep-runners require that they be exposed for a length of time to bright sunlight before they can glow properly down in the murky depths. In the darkening hours of dusk and even after nightfall, when the water surface is glassy smooth, I switch to surface lures. Surface or top-water lures attract fish not only with their shapes and actions but with the commotion they create when pulled across the water surface.

Torpedo-style surface lures have propellers on one or both ends. When the lure is pulled across the water, the propellers spin and buzz. I'm not sure what this action resembles to the fish, but fish strike torpedoes. Especially the tiny torpedoes, which, come to think of it, suggest sputtering moths trapped in the surface film.

What are known as popping lures all resemble frogs with wide-open mouths, and they float on the water in much the same way that frogs float. You fish a popping lure by using the tip of your rod more than your reel. Lift the rod tip and tug, making the lure lunge forward in the water. With each tug, the open mouth of the lure cups about a teaspoon of water, creating a loud *pop*! Reel

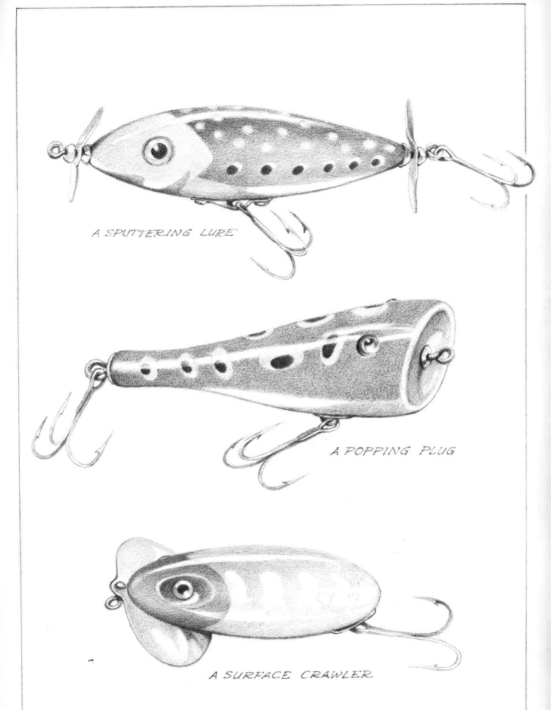

A SPUTTERING LURE

A POPPING PLUG

A SURFACE CRAWLER

THREE TYPES OF SURFACE LURES

in any slack line, lift your rod again, and tug. *Pop!* The noise nearly duplicates the sound of a frog plunging into water.

Some topwater lures are designed to be reeled in steadily rather than animated with the rod tip. When reeled slowly, they crawl along with tiny paddling strokes. I'm positive that fish take these lures for swimming mice.

Topwater lures will work only when the surface of the water is completely calm. In this quiet atmosphere, the disturbance the lure creates can bring in curious fish from considerable distances. Here's a secret: When topwater fishing, after each cast, wait until the water ring caused by the lure plopping down dissipates entirely. This will give fish that are off a little ways time to swim over to investigate the cause of the plopping sound. Once the water surface is again completely still, give the lure a twitch. You may get a strike right away. If not, start popping or reeling in whichever manner the type of lure calls for. At night, when the water is dead calm and black as ink, casting a surface lure into the darkness, hearing it plop down, working it back by feel and sound alone, all the while anticipating the loud *kerplunk* of a big bass gulping the lure down, is spooky. But what fun!

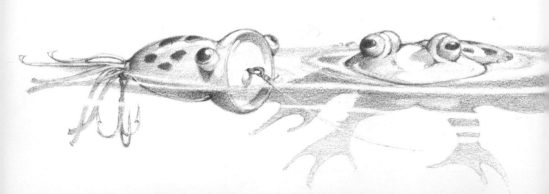

The most amazing nighttime fishing lure is the black rubber worm. It is amazing because it makes very little sound or commotion in the water, and I can't understand how the fish can see it. The worm must be black. Years ago when fishermen were just discovering the rubber worm as a fishing lure, a friend and I experimented using all the various colors of rubber worms on the market. For one whole summer, we fished day and night exclusively with rubber worms. We learned that a rubber worm hanging in the water like a real worm on a hook did not attract fish at all. We learned how to make the worms swim underwater by jerking them along and reeling up slack. Brown or natural-colored rubber worms made little impression on the bass we were fishing for. In fact, the more a rubber worm resembled a real worm, the less it attracted fish. Red, white, blue, and speckled rubber worms also made poor fish lures. The only two colors of rubber worms that consistently attracted fish were purple ones and black ones. The purple ones worked best during the day. The black worms worked best at night. The summer we experimented with rubber worms, this became the rule. We would fish the purple worms up to sunset, when suddenly they would stop producing fish strikes. Then, switching to black worms, we would catch fish through the twilight and on into the night.

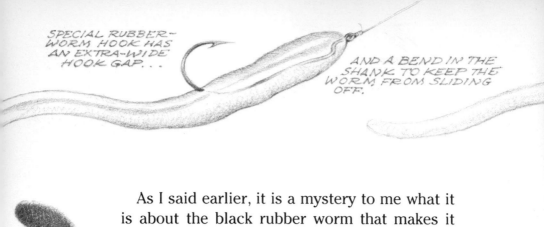

SPECIAL RUBBER-WORM HOOK HAS AN EXTRA-WIDE HOOK GAP...

AND A BEND IN THE SHANK TO KEEP THE WORM FROM SLIDING OFF.

As I said earlier, it is a mystery to me what it is about the black rubber worm that makes it such a great nighttime lure. Perhaps the black rubber, when seen against the undersurface of the water, silhouettes nicely in the dim moonlight.

Don't waste money on rubber worms sold already rigged with one, two, or three hooks. Buy the worms hookless by the handful or in a pack and add your own hooks. One large hook inserted in the nose of a rubber worm is all it needs to make it a fishing lure. To make the worm weedless, bury the point of the hook into the worm's rubber neck. If you wish to have the worm sink deep and bump the bottom, add a sliding sinker to the line just above the hook knot.

Fishing with a rubber worm involves different methods than does fishing with any other lure. You don't just reel in a rubber worm. You jerk it in, pausing between jerks to let the worm sink a few inches and undulate in the water. Reel up

A SLIDING SINKER KEEPS THE WORM DOWN DEEP WHILE ALLOWING IT TO DRIFT LIGHTLY IN THE WATER LIKE A SMALL EEL.

NO SNAP-SWIVEL

HOOK MADE WEEDLESS

what little slack there is in the line. Then jerk the worm again. Repeat all the way to the rod tip. When a fish bites a rubber worm, it takes a few seconds or more for the fish to get the whole worm into its mouth. Whenever I feel the unmistakable tug of a fish taking hold of a rubber worm, I stop reeling and count slowly: one, two, three, four. Then I rear back with my rod, pulling fast and hard on the line to set the hook in the fish's mouth. If the fish is a big one, you can feel its weight when you set the hook. Because rubber worms are soft and meaty, a fish hooked on one often does not realize it is hooked. It is an odd sensation, once you've hooked a big fish, to feel the fish swimming away slowly and nonchalantly as though nothing were wrong. Hang on, however! For when the fish suddenly gets the message from the drag of the line that it is indeed hooked, the action quickens. The fish tugs hard, dives down, and rockets back up, leaping clear of the water attempting to shake itself free.

This is the time when a fisherman must decide whether or not to keep the fish and eat it, or release it. Too much battling can weaken a fish to the point where it has little strength left to survive even if it is released. When I'm into a big fish, after a minute or so of fighting or after the fish leaps out of the water once, I make a decision to keep or not to keep. If I decide I want to bring the fish home for supper, I play it out until it rolls up to the surface exhausted. If I decide to release the fish, I try to reel the fish over to me while it is still strong, and as soon as I have it near enough, I lift the fish's head up out of the water. I carefully slide my fingers down the line to the lure and, as quickly and as gently as possible, remove the lure from the fish's mouth. The

Black Crappie ~ 7" length caught in choppy water ~ Lake Champlain ~ using a plain silver spoon

JSA 1990

fish, which had been temporarily immobilized by being held out of water, can then swim away. If it happens that I must grab hold of the fish's body in order to unhook it, I wet my hands first. Whenever you take hold of a fish with dry hands, you take the chance of rubbing off some of the fish's protective slime coating. And any place where the slime has been removed becomes more susceptible to disease.

Only keep a fish if you intend to kill and eat it. Never keep a fish only to show it to family or friends. Even a fish stored alive on a stringer kept in water, while the fisherman decides whether or not to release it, may become fatally damaged where the stringer passes through its gills.

Chapter 4
Lunkers on Light Line

*I*t was late in the afternoon, and though the sun was still hours from setting, the lake was already beginning its evening calm. Out in the deepest water, waves were settling to wavelets. Near the shore, wavelets were flattening out. A pair of swallows flew very low over the water, dipping their beaks to drink. I clambered down the rocky shore to the water's edge and, teetering on a seesaw boulder, made a short and clumsy cast. The red-and-white spoon hit the water about thirty feet out. I let it sink three feet before beginning my retrieve. I wasn't paying much attention to my line. I was watching the swallows.

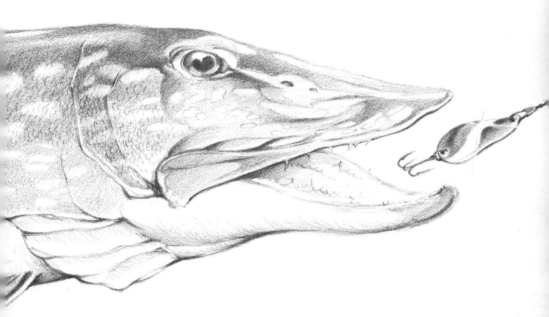

There were some people behind me walking along and we were exchanging greetings, when suddenly I felt the strong tug of a heavy fish. I raised my rod in a reflex action to the fish's pull and set the hook. The drag on my reel was set so that the fish was just barely stripping the line from the spool. This way no matter how heavy the fish was, it would not break my light line. Every chance I could, I reeled in slack line, bringing the fish a little closer. When the fish dove and tugged even harder, I loosened the drag a notch more, letting more line be pulled out. The fish slowed up, then ran parallel to the shoreline. Quickly, I retightened the drag and reeled in more slack. By keeping the line taut but not strained, I was able to keep the fish close to shore, so I could get a glimpse of what kind of fish it was. Finally the fish splashed on the surface. It was a handsome northern pike, as long as my arm and twice as strong.

Fish that run larger than the average size for their species are called *lunkers*. For example, sunfish on the average are a quarter to a half

Smallmouth Bass ~ unmeasured ~ caught in Kettle Pond ~ using a small silver spinner ~
JFA 1990

pound. A one-pound sunfish is considered a lunker. Largemouth bass average two pounds. Anything over three pounds falls in the lunker category. An averaged-sized pike weighs under seven pounds. Pike over seven pounds are lunkers.

There are lunkers, and then there are LUNK-ERS. LUNKERS are fish so far above average they make the lunkers look like squirts. I know of one smallmouth bass so incredibly large that I shudder whenever I cast to the weed bed where I first hooked the fish. It was midsummer and the lake was low. Weeds were choking the shallow water around the pond. I cast to the edge of one small weed bed. There was a great swirl in the water

around my line, and before I knew what had happened, I was into the monster. I watched in disbelief as my line was pulled so hard it felt like I had hooked an outboard motor. Then, before I could gather my wits about me, the fish exploded out of the pond. From its gills to its tail, the bass was at least three feet long! I watched wide-eyed as the fish splashed back down, broke my line, and got away. For years I hesitated to mention this fish to anyone, for fear I'd be accused of stretching the truth. But one day another fisherman who I know is not given to exaggeration confessed to me that he, too, had hooked the fish and could not believe its size. The fish snapped his bamboo rod in two. We both estimated our bass to be over three feet long, weighing somewhere around twelve pounds. Considering that smallmouth bass only average between two and three pounds, that twelve-pounder is indeed a LUNKER!

Most lunkers are lost because they startle the daylights out of the fishermen who hook into them. None of us expect to hook up with such big fish. To help compensate for the moment or two of panic one feels when a big fish takes a lure with a sudden rod-bending pull, make sure the drag on the reel is already loosened up enough so that the tug of a good-sized fish will peel off line rather than stretch and snap it. With the reel's bale in the locked position, take hold of the line between the reel and the first guide

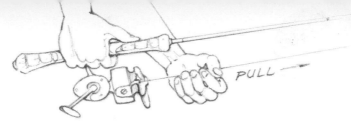

on your rod. Then **try** and pull the line from the
reel. If you cannot force the spool to turn and
peel off line, your **drag** is set too tight. A lunker
will snap a too-tight line in a few seconds. To
loosen the drag, keep pulling on the line and turn
the drag knob slowly, until the pressure of your
pull begins to turn the spool and strip off line.
Imagine your hand as a fish pulling on the line.
The harder the fish pulls, the more line strips off
the reel spool. With the drag set this way, it will
be virtually impossible for a fish, no matter how
large, to snap your line. Unless, of course, the
fish happens to be a sharp-toothed species, such
as a pike or a musky, in which case your line
may be sheared and broken. When I'm fishing in
water where pike live, I attach a twelve-inch wire
leader equipped with snap swivels to the end of
my monofilament line.

A lunker's first tremendous tug is only the start
of a lengthy and powerful battle. Big fish tend to
dive deep, then rocket back up. They drag your
line through brush and weeds, trying to snap it.
They run right at you in order to create enough
slack in the line so that they may shake free the
lure. Each of these maneuvers puts a great strain
on rod and line. Count on having to adjust the
drag throughout the fight: Loosen it a bit as
the fish pulls harder, and tighten up whenever the
opportunity presents itself for you to reel the fish
a little closer.

WIRE LEADER

Very large fish are difficult to take hold of unless they are tired. Whenever you catch a lunker, it is inevitable that you will have to tire it out before you can land it. A fish you wish to release may be a little too tired to swim away. Such a fish can be revived by holding it completely underwater, your hands gently cupping its body to keep the fish upright. Then, by moving the fish forward and backward in a gentle rocking manner, you will be forcing water into the fish's mouth and out through its gills. Little by little, the fish will resuscitate and show signs of returning strength. Eventually it will wiggle from your grasp and swim away. True, it will be worn from the ordeal. But it will live to continue terrorizing small fish and perhaps startle another fisherman another day.

On summer evenings, big fish that live in lakes and ponds spend the hot day in the cooler deep waters and, come evening, swim to the shallow waters to feed. Fishing for lunkers in shallow water is much more fun than deepwater fishing. In the shallows you can see where big fish are chasing schools of small fish. The water will be calm, and then suddenly it will be speckled with the tiny dorsal fins of small fish breaking through the surface in a panicky attempt to escape a big fish's jaws. Whenever you spot small fish behaving strangely, cast a flashy spinner or spoon into the crowd. Chances are you'll separate the monster from the masses.

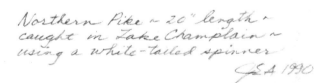

Northern Pike ~ 20" length ~ caught in Lake Champlain ~ using a white-tailed spinner
JEA 1990

Often you will first notice a big fish in shallow water just as it swirls on the surface, taking a floating insect or swimming frog. Before the swirling ring of water dissipates, cast your lure four or five feet beyond the swirl. As soon as it hits the water, begin reeling the lure back through the area in which the swirl occurred. If the fish is still in the vicinity and hasn't too much of a mouthful already, it will gobble up your lure in another swirling rise.

Large fish feeding near the shoreline hide in the weeds. In weedy shoreline water only a few inches deep, you can sometimes spot a large fish's back poking up out of the water. Lob your line toward the weeds so that the lure plops down into the water a foot or less away from the fish's hiding place. Then as soon as the lure hits the water, begin to reel it in. If nothing happens, do it again in the exact same way until the fish rushes out to seize the lure.

In lakes or ponds where there is little or no deep holes or cooler water, when the sun is high big fish will seek the cool shade beneath lily pads. The resting fish, though they are sluggish, will take a meal if it is served up to them. You can provide room service of a sort to skulking fish by casting a weedless rubber worm right on top of a lily pad. Let the worm stay still, draped over the lily pad, for as long as you can stand the suspense. Then jerk the worm off into the water. I've had largemouth bass take worm, pad, stem, and lily.

In streams, the lunkers tend to hang out under eroded banks or inside the flooded tunnels created by the weaving together of the roots of waterside trees. Most of these stream bullies rarely come out in daylight. They emerge to feed after dark. You can wait until dark to try your luck, or you can attempt to lure a big fish out of its lair during the day. Cast your brightest, flashiest spinner to a point upstream or downstream from a rooty spot and work the spinner by. Once you've passed the hot spot, cast and swim it by again. If you get no reaction, stand upstream from the rooty bank and cast downstream, reeling your spinner to a position right on the fish's doorstep. Then stop reeling and let the spinner hold, flashing in the current. If after five minutes nothing happens, give up. The fish won.

Chapter 5
Spinning from a Boat

I had been fishing from my twelve-foot boat, *Old Blue Oars*, all afternoon. It was time for a break—time to explore. I tilted the boat's engine to bring the prop up out of the water and, taking hold of the oars, rowed slowly, following the contours of the lake shore on my way to the mouth of Mud Creek. In the shallow water there was a firm gravel bottom. In some places fine, light-colored sand covered the gravel. There were trails in the sand. At first I thought the marks were caused by the keels of boats dragging on the bottom or by the ends of paddles and oars being used to pole boats along. However, the trails were erratic, crisscrossing and meandering over the sandy bottom. I stopped rowing and let the boat drift so that I could lean over and pick one trail out from the maze of trails and follow it with my eyes to its end. At the end of the trail, I found a freshwater clam! I followed another trail, then another. At the end of each there was a clam crawling along. The clams were moving

"Old Blue Oars"

so slowly they appeared to be stalled. As I was studying the clam trails and the clams, *Old Blue Oars* drifted me into the mouth of the creek. A dozen feet from the bow of the boat, a big fish swirled near the surface. In the midst of the swirl the broad dorsal fins of a largemouth bass poked up out of the water. The fins' sharp rays spread momentarily, then relaxed and flattened as the fish submerged and tore away in a straight line toward deeper water. The fish created a *V*-shaped wave on the water surface, the sight of which elevated my fisherman's blood pressure. But I was exploring, not fishing. I rowed up the creek, following a deep channel surrounded by a world of weedy water.

Lily pads covered most of the creek's surface, and the banks were not banks at all but flooded stands of cattails. The light green cattail stems poking up out of the dark, tea-colored water made a lovely scene. Suddenly a huge northern pike, startled by my oar dipping too close in the water, splashed around near the cattails and then shot out across the creek directly in front of the boat. The pike also created a deep *V*-shaped wave as it sped only inches below the water surface to a thick growth of water lilies. When the pike hit the lilies, it had to flip and flop on the surface, climbing and pushing its way through the tangle of stems and pads. Once the pike had broken through the vegetation, it dived deep and disappeared. It took a while for the water surface to calm. I glanced back toward the

CLAM TRAIL

lake. I had only rowed fifty feet up the creek and
had already seen things wild and wonderful. And
there were miles of creek yet to explore!

A boat can take you places you would never
be able to explore by just walking along the shore
or even wading in the water. In a large lake,
especially, a boat increases the area of water in
which a fisherman can fish. But with the added
mobility comes added challenge. Out in the open
areas of a lake, the fish may be down deep, con-
gregated around shoals or hanging out beneath
underwater ledges. Locating these fishy places
underwater takes a little skill in reading charts.
Getting to the places calls for strict safety mea-
sures. Open water can be dangerous.

Always wear a life preserver, even if the water is calm. Avoid standing up in a boat: It could capsize. Don't horse around in a boat or rock it intentionally in the water. Never venture out on windy days, when the water is rough, or during stormy weather. If you are out in a boat and the weather suddenly changes from calm to windy, or if you see a storm brewing off in the distance, come to shore as quickly as you can without racing dangerously. Remember that what may seem to be a big heavy boat to you on shore is only a small craft out in the open lake. My fishing boat, *Old Blue Oars*, is a twelve-foot aluminum skiff. It weighs over a thousand pounds. But out on the water, it bobs like a cork on the waves. I wouldn't want to be out on the lake in *Old Blue Oars* during high winds. I go out only when the water is calm, and even then, I stay to protected coves. *Old Blue Oars* seats only three comfortably and safely, with extra room enough for a

tiny fire extinguisher—for use in an emergency, when I'm running the gasoline-powered outboard motor—three float cushions in addition to the life jackets, tackle boxes, a short length of light line, called a "painter," to tie up to a dock, and a long length of heavy line attached to a six-pound anchor.

Small young children should never go out in a boat alone. Young fishing partners should always stay in sight and within easy swimming or wading distance of a parent or guardian on the shore.

When you are fishing from a boat, take care on each cast not to hook others in the boat. Try not to scrape your feet on the bottom of the boat. The sound created will reverberate underwater a great distance and frighten away the fish. You can talk all you want and even laugh out loud. Few airborne sounds ever reach, let alone startle, fish.

Chain Pickerel ~ 14" length
caught in weedy water ~
Lake Champlain ~ using a
gold-beaded spinner

JSD 1990

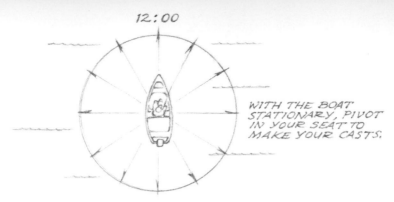

WITH THE BOAT STATIONARY, PIVOT IN YOUR SEAT TO MAKE YOUR CASTS.

When fishing from a boat, it is best to vary the direction of your casts to cover all the water that might hold fish. This way you won't be dragging your lure through the same fishless water over and over. Imagine your boat is resting dead center in a large circular clock face. Your first cast will be at 12:00. Reel in. Cast to 12:05. Reel in. Try 12:10 and reel in. Work your way all around the minutes of the clock until you get a strike. While you are casting around the clock, be alert for any sign of a fish feeding anywhere in the water—a dimple, a splash, a swirl, small fish scattering near the surface—and cast your lure into the action.

If there is a ripple in the water, pushing your boat ever so gently along, let the boat drift and fish the areas of water your boat slowly passes by. Always cast as far out from the boat as you can and work the lure all the way back to the boat. Sometimes fish will follow a lure right up to the side of a boat before attacking it. Drift-fishing is a most relaxing way to cover a lot of water. Just be aware how far your drift is taking you. If you are drifting in toward your home shore, sit back and enjoy the ride. If you are drifting outward, away from the shore, stop fishing every fifteen minutes or so to row back closer to home. A boat's drifting motion makes it difficult to properly manipulate and animate rubber worms and plugs. Spinners and spoons work nicely in the water, even though you are slowly drifting as you reel them in.

Another advantage of fishing from a boat, as opposed to fishing from shore or while wading, is that you can station a boat a little ways out from a shoreline, cast in to the shore, and reel your lure from the shallows out to deeper water. Fish in shallow water notice everything and are more likely to see and become interested in your lure plopping down. As you reel your lure from shallows to the deeper water offshore, a fish following it will become increasingly interested and then grow less inhibited as the water deepens, and it is more likely to strike the lure.

After hooking a fish and playing it to the side of the boat, the easiest way to subdue it is by using a net to gently scoop it out of the water. Keep it in the net while you carefully remove the lure's hooks from the fish's mouth. Try not to let the fish flop around too much in the bottom of the boat. As you remove the lure, keep the line to the lure slack. A taut line may suddenly snap the unhooked lure away from the fish and embed the hooks in your hand. Once the lure is removed, lift the fish in the net back over the side of the boat, making sure the net strings are well away from the fish's head so that it can easily swim out.

The longer your lure is in the water during the course of a day's fishing, the greater your chances are of catching fish. If you have decided to move on to try some new spot, don't just pull in your line and head off. Cover all the water along the way by trolling a spinner or spoon. Cast the lure about thirty feet behind the boat. As soon as the lure hits the water, prop your rod in a holder or against the gunwale of the boat and then begin rowing to the new fishing spot. The slightest motion of the boat, as long as the motion is steady, will keep the lure up off the lake bottom and impart lure action. As your spinner spins or your spoon wobbles underwater, your rod tip will throb steadily. If the throbbing tip is suddenly jerked toward the lure, quickly

ship oars and take hold of your rod. You may have picked up a hitchhiking lunker!

There are electric boat motors and small gas-powered outboards designed specifically for trolling. When I'm trolling I prefer to row. At sundown, when the surface of the lake flattens to a glass that mirrors the red-stained horizon, there is nothing so peaceful as rowing and trolling slowly along. Passing water tickles the splash guards on the sides of the boat. The dipping oars ripple the sunset's reflection. On the shore, bullfrogs bellow. A bittern calls. A swallow swoops down to the water, dipping its beak to drink. Bats appear and flap about on leathery wings through the cooling air. And the rod tip, darkly silhouetted against the sky, throbs to the rhythm of the lure working its wiles underwater.

Yellow Perch ~ 10" length ~ caught in Lake Champlain ~ trolling a small spinner in deep water
JEA 1990

Chapter 6
Some Final Thoughts

*N*ever underestimate a stream or pond. The smallest bodies of water are capable of supporting surprisingly large fish. I realized this years ago while fishing a neighbor's farm pond. The pond was perfectly round in shape and so small that, if you weren't careful, you could cast right over it into the grass on the opposite bank. The water was muddy from hooves of cattle walking in to drink and stirring up the pond's soft bottom. By working a spinner slowly through the deep water in the pond's center, I caught a few small bass, each only as long as my hand. Then something splashed nearby under the bank, and I walked over to the spot slowly, stepping softly so I would not vibrate the ground or shake the tall grasses overhanging the water.

It was too close quarters to properly use the spinner, so I changed to a long purple rubber worm. Then, reaching out so my rod barely poked over the edge of the bank, I let the worm drop—*plop!*—into the water just inches from the bank. The weight of the sinking worm peeled a little line off the reel. When the line stopped peeling off, I knew the worm had hit the muddy bottom. Motionless, I waited a minute. Then, just as I was about to begin jigging the line so that the rubber worm could rise off the bottom and dance in full view of whatever was lurking under the bank, something seized the worm with a strong pull that gradually increased in strength.

My rod bent and was dangerously close to breaking in two. The pulling didn't let up. My fingers fumbled around the reel to loosen the drag so some line would play out and relieve the rod of the relentless pressure of the pulling fish. The fish swam under the bank, and I walked along in the tall grass to keep up. The fish turned and swam faster the other way. I ran to keep up, reeling in a little line every chance I could. Finally, the fish swam out from under the bank and exploded on the surface, splashing and thrashing in the muddy water. It was a largemouth bass, three to four pounds, big enough to eat every other fish in the tiny pond and still be hungry!

Largemouth Bass ~ 12" length
caught in Lake Champlain ~
using a large spinner
JSA 1990

Spin-fishing using artificials such as spinners, spoons, plugs, or rubber worms is a way to catch fish without hooking them too far down in the mouth. This is why fish caught on artificials can be released with a minimum amount of harm done. It takes a little practice, however, to safely unhook a fish. This involves skillful handling of both the fish and the lure being removed. Most spinning lures have treble hooks, and the three sharp hook points are dangerous—especially when you are trying to remove them from a fish and the fish suddenly thrashes or jerks its head.

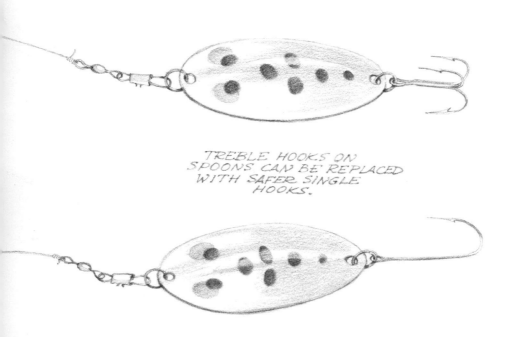

TREBLE HOOKS ON SPOONS CAN BE REPLACED WITH SAFER SINGLE HOOKS.

The safest way to grab hold of a treble-hooked lure is with a pair of needlenose pliers. Carry one in your tackle box. Using the pliers will keep your hand away from the hooks and any sharp teeth the fish may have.

To make hooks easier to dislodge, take time before you use a lure to flatten the hook's barbs by pressing on them with your pliers. Barbs only serve to make unhooking more difficult. If you keep your line taut, barbless hooks hold fish just as well as barbed hooks.

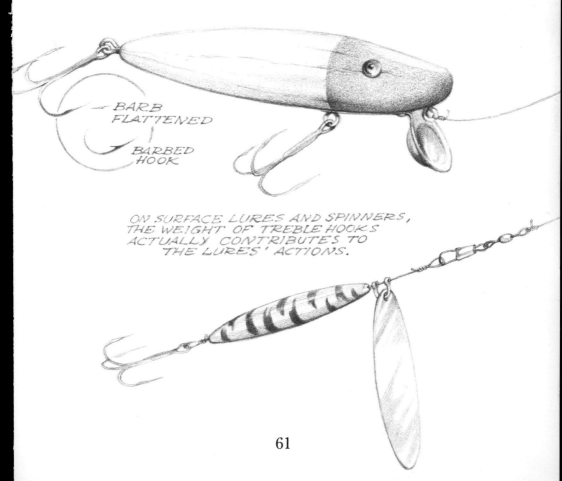

BARB
FLATTENED

BARBED
HOOK

ON SURFACE LURES AND SPINNERS,
THE WEIGHT OF TREBLE HOOKS
ACTUALLY CONTRIBUTES TO
THE LURES' ACTIONS.

When you go fishing, wear a hat to keep the sun off your head and to shade your eyes. In a small fishing boat, there is no place to escape the hot sun. A hat will keep your head and neck cool and protect you from heatstroke. Choose a fishing hat with dark-colored cloth under the brim. The dark material will absorb sunlight reflecting off the water. A light color under the brim will reflect the reflected light onto your face. Use a sun-blocking cream and put it on before you feel the sun burning your skin. You don't want a painful case of sunburn to ruin a good fishing

trip, do you? And the younger you start protecting your skin from the sun's damaging rays, the better. Use insect repellent to protect yourself from biting flies and ticks. When fishing from a grassy or brushy bank, stop every so often to check your clothing for ticks and remove any before they migrate to your skin. Ticks bite and suck blood and can transmit disease-causing organisms.

All of us who love to fish have a responsibility to preserve and protect the places where we do our fishing. Never litter a shore with lunch wrappers, lure packaging, or discarded fishing line. Monofilament line can be a death trap to small wild animals or birds that become tangled in it. Learn your state's fishing regulations. Don't hesitate to report those who catch fish illegally, litter, or dump pollutants in our waters. No one has the right to ruin and despoil the outdoors.

Pumpkinseed Sunfish ~ 7" length
caught in rocky shallows ~
Lake Champlain ~ using a bright
yellow-beaded spinner
JEA 1990

Finally, keep in mind that killing and eating some of the fish you catch is an important and altogether wholesome part of fishing. And yes, hooking and catching a fish, even if it is carefully released, still causes the fish grief and some slight harm. But to never catch any fish for fear of bothering or harming it, to never hold a glistening trout in your hand or to see up close the spectacular colors of a bluegill, to never know our native fish from direct experience would be disastrous. We cannot simply assume that all is well in the unseen underworlds of our lakes, streams, and rivers. And we certainly cannot afford to wait until fish are found floating dead along the shore for us to realize something is wrong with the water. Fishing keeps us informed and concerned about water quality. It adds to our understanding of the movements and population fluctuations of fish species. Fishing tunes us in to subtle changes in our environment. Most importantly, fishing takes us below the water surface and connects us to the life beneath.